Financial Wisdom: A Christian Perspective on Money and Debt

By : Robert W. Rushing, Jr.

William Wilberforce Press 2014

Many things have changed since biblical times. Surprisingly though, the early Christians faced many of the same problems we deal with today. As such, the bible has a great deal to say about the myriad of problems related to money, the acquisition of material things, and debt.

It is no secret that we live in a society suffering from considerable economic distress. Unfortunately, the church going Christian is in no way insulated from the consequences of this. To the contrary, he or she is arguably under even greater pressure, as he attempts to survive without compromising the values of his faith.

The reasons for economic hardship can be as diverse as humanity itself. For some, the problem is simply excessive spending. For others, an illness or accident results in job loss and catastrophic medical expenses. Some find their economic stability undermined by a divorce or custody battle. Whatever the reason, the problems are real, the consequences undeniable and serious.

The purpose of this short book is twofold. First of all, it offers some simple concepts and ideas that can quickly and dramatically improve your financial situation, without injury to the rights of others. Secondly, it will discuss the Christian ethics which apply to serious debt issues, and the options which are currently available to you.

The book is not intended to provide legal advice. As such, it will not address litigation tactics in debtor/creditor lawsuits or foreclosures, or how to apply for bankruptcy. These situations require fact specific advice, the kind that can only be obtained by talking to a lawyer. If you are involved in such a situation, be aware that time is not on your side. You may be seriously and irreparably prejudicing your rights by failing to do so.

However, this book can go a long way towards keeping you out of financial trouble, and offer some solutions to common financial problems. Good habits, repeated on a regular basis, lead to increasingly better results. This principle works whether the goal is spiritual, health oriented, or financial.

CHAPTER ONE

WHAT THE BIBLE SAYS ABOUT MONEY

The Bible teaches us that an excessive desire for material things and money is destructive. This is a point emphasized throughout. If you were to ask random people on the street to recite something from the Bible, the response would most likely be this:

"The Lord is my shepherd. I shall not want.

He maketh me lie down in green pastures,

He leadeth me in the path of righteousness for his name's sake,

Yea, though I walk through the valley of the shadow of death,

I will fear no evil, for thou art with me,

Thy rod and thy staff they comfort me."

Psalms 23:1-4 (KJV)

Some, but substantially fewer, would recollect the next verse, which goes as follows:

"Thou preparest a table before me in the presence of mine enemies.

My cup runneth over. "

Without a doubt, the verse reminds us to refrain from obsessions over worldly things, and the troubles of an uncertain world. However, to my mind, it is often misinterpreted. Some believe that these verses, among the most comforting and beautiful words in the English language, indicate that our needs will be provided for regardless of our actions, provided only that we have faith. By this logic, sufficient prayer and sincere belief would result in winning the lottery.

However, the verses must be taken in context. The language begins by describing the Lord as "my shepherd." This makes his role something more than a passive, undemanding provider. The shepherd does attend to his sheep and care for their needs, but he also makes demands. He requires them to follow his lead, traveling when and where he leads them, resting when he instructs them to rest, and eating and drinking when, what, and to the extent that he instructs them to.

My point is this. The principle of the twenty third Psalm is not that those who believe will be provided for. Rather, it is that those who believe **and follow** the word of God in their day to day lives will be provided for. This means that the believer must follow God's word, which instructs believers to work hard, and maintain a high standard of character and ethics, among other things, to reap the benefits described in Psalms.

For example, in Proverbs 27:12, we find the following advice.

"A prudent man sees evil and hides himself, the naïve proceed and are punished."

To my mind, this is among the handful of most important verses in the Bible. It requires us to question the circumstances and individuals around us, weighing their motivations, their credibility, and the potential effects of their actions upon yourself and those to whom you are responsible.

For example, you would obviously want to avoid cooperating with a person who wanted you to assist him in illegal acts in order to make money, by stealing for example. However, you might also want to consider the effects of taking money from an outwardly benevolent source, such as government. Are you empowering a third party to make decisions which might ultimately affect your ability to practice your faith?

In Proverbs 13:16 the point is restated as follows: "A prudent man acts with knowledge but a fool displays his stupidity."

As such, it is fair to say that God expects us to be diligent and careful in our financial dealings. Unfortunately, in the increasingly complicated world in which we live, this can be easier said than done. Many of us are genuinely afraid to address issues related to our day to day finances, let alone long term planning for vital things such as the education of a child, or retirement.

Fortunately, the Bible also reminds us that we are not alone. In Proverbs 16:9, it is noted that :

"A man's heart deviseth his way; but, the Lord directeth his steps."

You are not alone in doing this important work, no more than you are in any other aspect of your life. There is valuable guidance in the Bible for those who seek it, and even more to be found in prayer. It is not a sign of a lack of faith to prepare and plan for the future, or to make preparations for hard times. Rather, it is simply an act that follows the instruction provided to you as a believer.

"Go to the ant, O sluggard, observe her ways and be wise, which, having no commander,

Overseer or ruler, yet it shares its provisions in summer and gathers its food at harvest."

Proverbs 6:6-8.

Like the simplest of God's creatures, we must work, share, and save. These characteristics were put in the ant, and likewise in man. These traits are a gift from the almighty that will in time of need provide. They are the kindly staff of a shepherd, leading us to the table.

The remainder of this book is intended as a tool to help you deal with some common financial issues. Some of the content consists of simple money saving tips. Elsewhere, it will address serious legal problems such as eviction, foreclosure, and automobile repossession. Always, the intent will be to keep within the spirit of these verses.

CHAPTER TWO

SURVIVAL TACTICS FOR THE SPIRIT AND PURSE

As we have seen, the Bible makes it clear that a Christian must pay his lawful debts. However, it also condemns unfair dealing by creditors, and particularly outright theft. In no way does it require a Christian to submit to the loss of his worldly goods by those who are not entitled, or to live in poverty. Rather, you must arm yourself with knowledge, make intelligent decisions about money, and use the law and whatever other means are available to safeguard the financial well-being of yourself and your loved ones.

So how is this principle translated into practical decision making? It is necessary to learn and apply some simple, common sense rules. For example:

1. Painful and frustrating as it can be, take the time to do a budget. Calculate a monthly average of the money coming in to the household. Do not forget to include income that is not derived from your principle source, such as interest from a bank account.

2. Then (and this is the part that hurts) start to itemize the bills. There are many good computer programs and applications designed to help you to do this. However, the process is actually relatively simple. On the sheet of paper, right down the monthly amount of any payment made by you on a regular basis in the following areas:

Mortgage payment or Rent

Automobile payment

Credit card payment

Child support if applicable

Utilities including electric, cable, water, Internet, etc.

Entertainment expenses (this can include movies or movie rentals, lessons, sporting activities, or anything else you or a family member does for fun)

Clothing expenses (these should be averaged on a monthly basis)

Unsecured debt not payable on a monthly basis (this usually includes personal loans from family or friends and should be averaged on a monthly basis)

Medical or dental insurance

Insurance including homeowner's, rental, automobile, or liability

Work related expenses such as uniforms, professional liability insurance, etc.

Include any other expense which occurs on a regular basis, such as an ongoing debt being paid on a monthly basis.

 Most people would rather be shot than look at these numbers. The reason is that truth hurts. Still, it is a first step towards making things better if, like most people, you find yourself amazed that the two ends meet.

 If you have substantial credit card debt, you will easily spot the iceberg up ahead, ready to sink your ship. Take your latest statement, and check out how much of the payment is applied to interest. This is money that is going out of your monthly budget, and providing nothing in the way of goods and services.

 This is the fat on your budget. Just like fat on your body, it is making you work harder every day to survive. Just like the process of losing weight, the hard part is getting started. Once you commit to paying more than the minimum payment, and retiring your credit card debt, the rewards will rapidly follow. Soon, there will be more money to spend on what you want or need, and a sense of pride that can be better than anything you will find in the store.

Now, look at where the rest of the money is going. If you're honest, you'll see a fair amount of unnecessary spending. A lot of this is what I would call comfort spending, which is fine in moderation. Some people go out after a bad day and buy a pair of shoes, jewelry, or fishing equipment. In my case, I always end up in a book store or a music shop. I spend a relatively insignificant amount of money and walk out with a bag in my hand, feeling better.

The important thing is to track this kind of spending, set a limit, and stick to it. You might also want to keep in mind the other problems that come from a habit taken too far. I now have a room full of bookshelves, stuffed, leaning sideways and threatening to collapse to the floor. I could spend the rest of my life reading and listening, and never get through it all. Someday, I know this stuff will have to go, but I dread the job.

Lastly, when it comes to the essentials, shop around. For example, automobile, life and health insurance rates vary constantly, as do your needs. You might be carrying too much life insurance because you had minor children in the home at the time now grown and raised. This might be a reason to adjust the coverage. You might also consider reducing the home insurance on a property that has depreciated in value, or when mortgage is paid in full.

Of course, there are just as many reasons to increase coverage. Consider the nature of the loss you are protecting yourself against, and the extent of the coverage. Also, check competitor rates for the same coverage. There are multiple sites on line which allow you to do this easily.

The same principles can be applied to other bills. For example, do you really need the most expensive cable plan if you can access most of the programming on a cheap alternative such as NetFlix? Do you cut off lights and adjust the thermostat when you leave your home?

In the worst case scenario, weigh the relative consequences of failure to pay your various bills. You might find that the creditors who are the most aggressive about demanding payment (such as credit card companies) will do the least damage should you fail to pay. Once they have reported you to the credit agencies their only remedy is to file a file a lawsuit which they know to be unlikely to get them paid.

This is not as painful as losing essential utilities such as electricity or water, repossession of a vehicle, eviction, or foreclosure. Regardless of the threatening letters and hostile phone calls, look at the consequences of default and commit your resources accordingly.

Of course, these are your lawful debts. As we have discussed, the Bible tells us to pay them. However, where the capacity to pay is limited, it is important to make the right choices. Later, when the situation improves, those who are owed should be paid in full.

Some creditors are more motivated to work with you, and some are under considerable pressure to do so. For example, a bank is very reluctant to repossess a car. Repossessions are not profitable for them. The car will be sold at auction for pennies on the dollar. The debtor is angry about the loss of the vehicle, and so not usually inclined to hitch a ride or walk to the bank to make his monthly loan payment.

As such, there is an opportunity to negotiate. Look at the budget you have already completed, and calculate a loan payment you could make comfortably. Then call the bank and offer to pay one half of that amount. Keep in mind how a negotiation works. The bank will take your initial offer as an invitation to negotiate, and will make a counteroffer. The idea is to forge an agreement at somewhere near the amount that you are comfortable paying. Of course, if they readily agree to the lower amount, so much the better.

If you pursue this strategy, insist on a letter or e mail confirming the agreement. The honesty of banks and bank employees has been called into question since the time of Bonnie and Clyde. If you do not protect yourself, you run the real risk of the bank simply pocketing your payment, applying it to interest owed, and ignoring any verbal agreement with you.

Never send large amounts of money to a debtor without knowing three things: 1) the total amount you owe, 2) the amount of the payment to be applied to principle, and to interest;

3) the exact terms of any modification agreement that has been discussed.

Be aware that if you are negotiating a change in the contract, the law of your state may require that the new agreement be put in writing in order for it to be enforceable. If you are in doubt about this, either insist on a written agreement (after all, what could be the harm of putting the deal in writing), or consult an attorney.

Creditors who offer essential services such as utilities are often required to negotiate with customers in hardship. Many power companies offer an automatic extension of thirty days on a late bill merely for the asking. All the customer has to do is call the company, follow the voice mail directions, and answer a few questions.

Of course, utilities exist in service of the first and foremost essential, the home. Many of the great names in American finance benefited from a huge government bailout only a few years ago. This was required to rescue them from the consequences of widespread questionable or outright fraudulent practice in the area of home loans. Billions of dollars in taxpayer money were handed over with no strings attached to save them from default.

Under the circumstances, one would expect financial institutions to show similar compassion towards hard pressed debtors. Nothing could be farther from the trust. Banks have employed rigid and unyielding tactics, pressuring individuals into foreclosure where this could easily have been avoided. The result has been intervention by state and federal government.

CHAPTER TWO: BANKS AND DEBT COLLECTORS

As we have seen, there are two general rules that apply when income is insufficient to pay all bills or even essential bills. First, pay for necessities first. For example, if the credit card payment is due, and the mortgage is also due, ignore any threats/demands by the credit card company or collection agency, and keep the roof over your head. This is a no brainer.

Secondly, do your best to communicate with the creditor you cannot pay and suggest terms that are workable for you. You will never hear this from a debt collector, or see it in a letter from your credit card company, but they have strong reasons to cooperate.

This is especially true where the creditor holds what is called unsecured debt. In other words, they do not have a legal right to take any of your property if you fail to pay, unlike for example, the bank that holds the mortgage on your house or the title to the car. This is usually the situation with credit card debt, among other things.

Unsecured debt can be easily discharged in bankruptcy under certain circumstances. If that were to happen, the credit card company would receive payments in the range of ten percent of the total debt owed or less. Absent other circumstances, they are much better off negotiating a short term reduction in the payment than have you go in default and lose practically everything.

Is your credit rating a factor in all of this? It is in a way. Your credit history is still being documented, and the late or missed payments hurt. However, at this point, the damage has probably already been done. You may have a hard time accessing credit in the future. However, you can probably avoid being sued, without surrendering money needed for necessities.

If you do decide to negotiate, there are a few things you should keep in mind before picking up the phone and calling the creditor. First of all, everything is recorded. Any statement you make can be used against you later in a court of law. For this reason, you must avoid admitting to the validity of the debt. Even if you think it is a legitimate debt, there may be defenses or issues you are not yet aware of.

Secondly, you will not be provided a copy of the recorded conversation, unless of course you are sued and obtain it through discovery prior to trial. This means that you will not be in a position to prove the particulars of any agreement you work out. Insist on a written document verifying all particulars of your agreement before you send in the first dollar.

Again, we all know the major role that the banks and particularly their mortgage divisions had in economic collapse of a few years ago. Much of the conduct in question was motivated by pure, heartless greed. Do not make the mistake of assuming that the person on the other line shares your Christian ethics.

I have heard many horror stories through the years from people who claimed, believably, that they had worked out a deal with the bank to save their home, car, or credit. However, when they sent in their hard earned money, the bank pocketed it, applied it to interest, and went ahead with foreclosure, repossession, or whatever other plans they had for the poor soul.

Thirdly, ask to view the original copies of all documents related to the debt. This is especially important when dealing with home mortgages. As you may remember, during the mortgage boom that occurred several years ago, many documents were improperly executed, making the contracts invalid and stopping a foreclosure in its tracks. If the Bank is reluctant to produce the original documents, assume that where there is smoke there is also fire. A false or facsimile signature on the mortgage or note could literally save your home. Consult an attorney who can help you get the original documents.

Finally, guard yourself against abuse. The Federal Fair Debt Collections Practices Act protects consumers against certain conduct by debt collectors. This would include abusive, hostile or threatening language, calling at late hours, calling repeatedly, or misrepresenting the legal remedies available to them.

The act provides for the awarding of actual damages, punitive damages (a remedy that allows a jury to increase a cash award to punish a defendant for particularly bad conduct), and importantly, attorney's fees, expenses and costs. In the current economic and political environment, increasingly more attorneys are willing to file these cases on a contingency fee basis, meaning they get paid only if you do.

The act also gives the debtor a way to stop calls from debt collectors. The creditor simply has to write a letter informing the debt collector that he or she does not wish to be contacted further. After receiving the notice, the creditor has the right to make one additional contact, to inform the debtor of the legal action which might be taken. After that, further contact is a violation of the act, and the creditor has the right to sue.

The letter should be sent certified mail, return receipt requested. It should specifically state that it is a notice under the Federal Fair Debt Collection Practices Act required the creditor to cease contact. If there has been abusive language towards you or others, mention this. Likewise, if there other inappropriate conduct, such as calls late at night or early in the morning, or calls to third parties, mention this specifically. Include your account number in the correspondence. Keep a copy of your letter and certified mail receipt in a file.

It is also important to be aware of the length of time that has passed since a debt was incurred. Commonly, many businesses sell their old accounts to collection firms for pennies on the dollar. These firms acquire and collect old debt as a business. They tend to be the source of much of the abusive conduct which has given debt collection such a bad name.

Often, years have passed before such firms acquire an account and attempt collection. For this reason, their first order of business is often simply to get you to acknowledge owing the money. In many states, a verbal acknowledgement that the debt is legitimate is enough to allow the collector to file suit, even if the statute of limitations has already passed.

Never acknowledge owing money on an account to a debt collector over the phone. The conversation is recorded, and your statements may have serious financial consequences. Until you have obtained legal advice, you have every right to question whether, and to what extent, you owe the money.

There are a few other liability issues which seem to cause confusion. Here are short answers to some frequently asked questions:

1. You do not owe money to a creditor simply because your current or former husband or wife has incurred a debt. You must sign a contract or execute an agreement in your own right, or cosign as a guarantor, for this to be the case.

2. You do not assume the debts of your husband, wife, or child when they die. The estate of the deceased love one may be liable, if a proper claim is filed on a timely basis. Such a debt can take precedence over the interest of the heirs, and may be paid from money that would otherwise be distributed to heirs. However, your personal assets are safe unless you have signed a document yourself securing or guaranteeing the debt.
3. You are not liable for the debts of a corporation of which you are a member, or a shareholder, including a limited liability corporation. The corporation is considered a fictitious person under the law, able to contract and pay debts in its own right. Of course, banks and credit agencies know this, and will ordinarily make individual members of a small corporation co-sign before any credit is extended.
4. However, if you are a member of a business partnership, you may very well be liable for debts incurred by your partners, even without your knowledge. The issue turns on the language of the partnership agreement, which is a contract between yourself and the other partners. These agreements often grant a single individual broad power to spend, borrow, or otherwise pledge the money of the other partners. As a result, few people enter into this kind of business relationship. Beware of informal business situations in which the checkbook is informally passed back and forth, and open accounts in multiple names that are seldom reviewed.
5. There are many contracts, even if agreed to by the parties that are nevertheless unenforceable. These would include contracts in which one of the parties in under age, contracts in which one of the parties is mentally incompetent, certain contracts which are invalid as against public policy (for example, contracts dealing with illegal subject matter), and contracts which are required to always be in writing and properly witnessed (for example, a contract to purchase real estate.)
6. With exceptions which vary from state to state, an oral contract can be enforced. The most common exceptions are any agreement relating to any interest in real estate, and contracts that exceed a certain maximum monetary value.

These are general guidelines intended to help you determine whether or not you legitimately owe money to a creditor. If you believe you have a valid defense, and a lawsuit is filed against you, seek legal help immediately. The law in the area is relatively complicated, with lots of traps for the unwary.

If your exposure is for a limited amount of money, try to find an attorney willing to handle the matter for a flat fee instead of a billable hourly rate. This is also an area of the law in which most community legal assistance programs are pretty well versed. Seek them out and ask for their help. Even if you do not qualify for representation, they are at least a good and willing source for information and advice.

CHAPTER THREE: EVICTION AND FORECLOSURE

One of the basic principles of human nature is that when a person acts out of fear, he or she is likely to make mistakes. There are few situations more likely to cause fear than the prospect of losing a home. The rest goes without saying.

Out of panic, many people simply leave the home at the first threat of a foreclosure or eviction, or immediately after being served with legal papers. This is a huge mistake. Before subjecting yourself to an uncertain future, you owe it to yourself and those who depend on you to make an informed decision.

Chances are that you are facing this situation for the first time. If so, you are unlikely to know what questions to ask. The issues related to a foreclosure are much different from those involved in an eviction. However, there are some constants on the "To Do" list. They are as follows:

1. If you have been served with legal papers, read them slowly and carefully. There is some essential information that needs to be obtained immediately.

    a. You must note and write down the date and time the papers were given to you, as well as by whom. If they were not given to you personally, note the name of the

person who accepted the papers and the address at which they were served.
   b. Look carefully on the papers for a date, time and location of the hearing at which you must appear. You are required to be provided notice of any hearing, ordinarily by having the notice delivered to you personally or through the mail, but sometimes by publication in a local newspaper.
   c. Look for any language in the documents that provides a deadline for responding to the papers, and indicating to whom the response should be sent.

2. If you do not understand the papers, make it your business to get the help of someone who will. This could be a private attorney, or alternately, a community legal assistance group or court employee. Do this immediately. Often, you will only be provided a few days' notice prior to a hearing, or require you to take other action relatively quickly in order to avoid losing your case before it starts. Whatever you do, do not put the documents aside and forget about them, as is so tempting to do.

3. Once you understand the documents create a "To Do" list of tasks that must be completed before you go to court. This could include obtaining proof of payment (such as cancelled checks) from a bank, collecting important documents such as mortgages, notes, leases, or correspondence, or simply going out and hiring a lawyer.

4. Take a calendar, and schedule times to act on the items on the "To Do" list, giving yourself a reasonable amount of time to complete each task, but soon enough to allow for the expected problems and delays involved in doing something unfamiliar and important. Once you have set these down on paper, stick to them.

The simpler of the two actions to address is eviction. Since these cases involve rental properties, they avoid the more important and complicated issues of title and ownership to land. As such, the legal process moves much more quickly.

This fact is both blessing and curse. While it is intended to benefit the property owner, the short, quickly scheduled hearing can be an advantage, if you are prepared.

It is essential that you come to some reasonable conclusions as to how the eviction will resolve itself. The key questions are firstly do you expect to be removed from the property? Secondly, if the answer is yes, how soon will this happen?

There are several reasons that an eviction might be stalled or even prevented. Many of these relate to legal issues which vary from state to state. However, most of the keys to a defense lie in the lease itself. Chances are you did not read it in its entirety when it was signed. Most people never do. Almost certainly, it is loaded with terms intended to protect the landlord as opposed to the tenant.

However, the mere fact of setting out an agreement in writing has its advantages. The lease and applicable law will set up a fairly rigid process for the removal of a tenant. Usually, this will involve a certified or registered letter being mailed to you, advising you of your rights through language prescribed by statute. The letter informs the tenant that rent payments are delinquent, or that there are other issues which could result in removal from the property.

The letter must be sent a certain number of days prior to the filing of an eviction action. It is typically called a "Right to Cure" letter.

The tenant must then be provided with a certain number of days advance notice of the court hearing. This is often five to ten days. If the notice is not timely, and there is not sufficient legal proof of delivery, this is a defense to the eviction.

There are several additional issues which might be raised successfully. For example, the parties might have effectively changed the terms of the lease, by performing their contractual obligations in a way other than what it describes.

The fact that one of the one of the parties has, for example, allowed payments to be made late, might waive the enforceability of a the requirements of the lease.

If this is your situation, you should first review the original lease before appearing in court. It might contain language specifying that any modification of the agreement must be in writing, signed by both parties to the lease, and witnessed. This is a standard clause in most commercial leases, but often missing in agreements written informally by parties not represented by attorneys.

Also, be aware that lease agreements intended to last over a one year are required to be in writing to be valid in most states. The rule also applies to changes to a lease. However, I have seen judges accept text messages, e mails, or informal notes made on an envelope and signed by both parties.

There is also some very helpful law in this area. It can be successfully argued that if an agreement has been performed by one party, then the other party is bound to perform his end of the bargain. In law school, this is called equitable estoppel, but it is really just a simple fairness argument.

Another argument that can win an eviction action relates to failure of the landlord to provide things essential to the agreement. For example, the law provides to every tenant what is referred to as a warranty of habitability. Again, this is a technical term for a simple, commonsense notion.

The warranty of habitability requires the landlord to give the tenant what he or she is paying for. This means that the rented property must be in a condition to allow the tenant to use it for its intended purpose. This would require things like properly operating climate control, running water, and other essentials. If the landlord has notice of such problems, failure to make repairs can be a defense to an action to collect rent. If conditions on the property are poor enough, a judge can rule that the tenant has been "constructively evicted" from the property, and therefore owes the landlord nothing.

A foreclosure action is typically a more high stakes game. This is to be expected, since the party being removed from the property is in the process of purchasing and occupies as an owner. He or she can be expected to have a far greater financial and emotional investment in the property in question.

The eviction process begins long before papers are filed. There will usually be letters, phone calls, and other contacts advising you of the delinquent status of the account. As unpleasant as it may be, it is important to review and save all communications. These will contain the numbers as to what you owe, at least as interpreted by the bank or finance company.

The numbers should be reviewed and compared to your own records. At this point, you should set up a file with proof of every payment made, whether it is the monthly mortgage payment, insurance, tax, or other expenses.

Notice that the letters often state that the amounts alleged as owed will be considered undisputed if you do not respond. This is not legally binding on you. However, you should write and dispute any amounts which are excessive or incorrect, sending your response certified. The act of doing so will create several advantages and opportunities later on.

Also, be aware that the people who will contact you for a bank or finance company have differing levels of authority within the company, and too often, questionable business ethics. Most importantly, understand that if you offer to make a payment on an account which is seriously delinquent, the bank will gladly take the money. However, a promise that the account will be restore to good standing should be taking with skepticism unless the agreement is put in writing.

 Plenty of times, I have had clients come to my office with a cancelled check written to a bank or finance company in the amount of a monthly payment or two. The check was quickly cashed, the funds applied to interest and penalties, and the foreclosure action filed as if nothing had happened.

If you are looking to save your property by catching up payments, get a specific agreement in writing. By specific, I mean the following:

1. It should specify your name, account number, and the address of the property.
2. It should specify the precise amount of the delinquency in the account; in other words, exactly how far behind you are as of the date of the agreement.
3. It should specify a payout as of the date of the agreement, letting you know how much money you owe on that particular date.
4. If you are going to make the payment at some time in the future, it should indicate for how long the figures in the document will be accurate. (Keep in mind that interest is calculated on a daily basis, as are penalties. You do not want to create a problem with the agreement by paying an amount that does not cover the delinquency.)
5. It should be signed (not just facsimile signed) by an agent of the creditor bank or finance company who indicates that he or she has the authority to make the agreement.
6. If you have any questions or concerns about the content, make the relatively small investment necessary to retain an attorney for the purposes of reviewing the document and assisting with the transaction.
7. Either way, make numerous copies of the documents involved and DO NOT LOSE THEM.

The farther along you go in the process, the more difficult things become. If you have been served with foreclosure papers, and you can afford to do so, retain an attorney immediately. The issues related to defending a foreclosure case are too complicated for an untrained person to handle alone.

Time is not on your side. Far too many people attempt to handle important legal issues of this nature on their own, later realizing they are in over their head. By the time they take the papers to an attorney, serious and often irrevocable mistakes have been made. There are situations in which it is possible to be your own lawyer, and do so effectively.

However, as the stakes get higher, this becomes a bad idea. Saving your home is, for most people, a very high stakes game.

If you retain an attorney, there are a few simple rules you should follow. Expect to sign a written retainer agreement. If at all possible, attempt to negotiate a flat fee for the service. This might appear to be more expensive initially. However, paying for an attorney by the hour adds up in a hurry.

Most attorneys will agree to accept a lump sum payment, especially where it is going to be paid up front. Also, unless you already have a relationship with an attorney, it is best to shop around. Set up consultations with two or three before making a decision, if there is time.

If you have no other options, file a responsive pleading on your own. Do not be intimidated by the imposing look and feel of legal documents. It is not necessary to exactly duplicate the obscure forms and legal captions. You need merely to prepare and properly file a document that indicates your position as to the issues presented in the legal documents served on you.

The technicalities of pleadings in a foreclosure action are set by state law. The information you need should be readily available on line, from the clerk of the court in which the case is filed, or by a neighborhood legal assistance program.

However, you should make a real effort to get as much information as possible about state and local procedures at this point, especially if you are forced to go it alone. This must be done immediately, as the time to respond to pleadings in a case like this ranges from twenty to thirty days, not long considering the stakes.

If you find yourself completely lost and out of time, just file something. Even if you simply write a letter explaining your side of the case, and send it to the court clerk and opposing counsel, you are far better off than you would be by doing nothing.

Most courts will treat the letter, if responsive to the content of the complaint, as a pleading. This means that you would not be held in default. In sports terms, this means that you stay in the game, instead of losing the cased right then and there. It buys you valuable time and gives you options.

You now have two major objectives if the goal is to keep your home. The first one is to slow down the process and make sure the case is decided in the right forum. Simply, this translates into getting the case off of the non-jury roster (where it will be decided by a Judge) and on to the Jury roster (where it will be decided, of course, by ordinary citizens from your community).

There are at least two reasons for this. The first involves the nature and purpose of the non-jury process. Basically, it is intended to process claims quickly, moving them through the roster through brief, rapidly set hearings. If you are trying to stay in your home, this is clearly not in your interest.

Secondly, because of its nature, the non-jury court tends to be a cozy forum for the attorneys who appear there frequently. Most of the hearing are uncontested, and essentially involve one of a short list of attorneys appearing with a huge stack of files.

The short factual presentation is completed in almost ritual fashion, almost identical in every case. Once in a while, the attorney and the judge will take a break and make small talk, catching up on gossip and current events. They do this on a regular basis, and are comfortable with each other.

This is generally not an atmosphere in which a stranger with a contested issue will find a sympathetic ear. More likely, the warmth of the room will be temporarily stifled by the intrusion, and he or she will be allowed to address the court briefly. The stranger will then be sent away, having been told that the defense is invalid, or that an order will be issued later. While there are exceptions, the stranger has a slim chance of success.

PART TWO: GETTING THE CASE TO A JURY

What you need is a forum that makes the bank, or the finance company, uncomfortable. Fortunately, in the United States, such a thing exists. It is a group of citizens, from all walks of life, with no ties to the bank or to you. They are rounded up against their will every few weeks, and made to sit and listen to cases. While most of them, truth be told, would rather be someplace else, they have no choice but to hear your case. This group is called a jury.

The members of a jury are people like you. Many have had sour experiences with banks, finance companies or credit card companies and also long memories. Some keep up with the news and recall how the financial misdeeds of the mortgage industry nearly collapsed the nation's economy a few years back, and the multi- billion dollar bailout the guilty received. The people seeking to foreclose on your house are aware of this, and it worries them.

So how do you get the case to a jury? First of all, you must file what is called a counterclaim, which essentially means that you ask the court for an award of damages of your own against the bank. Even if you have your own attorney, he or she might not consider this option, instead planning to make a defense in the non-jury setting. However, unless there is some compelling reason not to do so, a counterclaim should be strongly considered.

The counterclaim would have to be based upon the particular facts of the case. However, here are some common facts which could be the basis of a counterclaim.

1. You have not been provided an accounting of your payments as requested or required by law.
2. Your payments have not been properly credited by the bank.
3. The bank or finance company agreed to a modification of the contract, such as a temporary

reduction in payment, and is now failing to abide by the agreement.
4. You were not competent at the time of signing of the note, mortgage and contract.
5. You were misled to the point of fraud as to the content of the documents you signed.

Besides putting the issues of your case in the hands of people like you, instead the bank's friend, it has other advantages. It slows down the foreclosure process dramatically. The non-jury case will be resolved in most jurisdictions in as little as two to six months after which time you will be packing your bags. The jury case, by contrast, will generally last over a year, often considerably longer than that. This is valuable time that can be used for multiple purposes.

Also, the change allows time for fact finding and preparation. As I have mentioned, one of the many problems with the mortgage boom of a few years ago was sloppy and often fraudulent paper work. Many of the banks and financial institutions do not have the original documents such as the contract, note, and mortgage which commit you to the payment. Some of the documents were never signed, or were signed by fictitious parties.

If this is the case, there is a major, probably fatal problem with the contract. This would ordinarily not mean that you get a free house, but it would mean that the payment schedule and other requirements of the contract, such as the default provisions, are null and void. The bank would not be able to take your home based on the contract. Instead, the court would have to decide what is fair under the circumstances, and create a financial arrangement that is fair to both parties.

As such, you have to insist on reviewing the originals of all documents. If the opposing attorney squirms at this request, assume that there is smoke where there is fire. You can require the bank to produce these documents by several means which are essentially consistent in all federal and state courts.

The simplest is to issue a subpoena duces tecum, which is a form requiring a party to a lawsuit to appear and produce a specified list of items or documents. Again, this is beyond what a non-attorney would be comfortable doing, in that there are technical issues to service of the subpoena, and the list of items to be included will vary from case to case. However, if you are stuck doing it alone, at a minimum request the **original** Contract, Finance Agreement, Note, and Mortgage. You would request that these be brought to court be an agent or employee of the bank or finance company with custodial control over such documents.

While you are at it request all correspondence including e mails, texts, and letters, related to the account. Opposing counsel will object, calling it work product, or claiming that it is protected by attorney client privilege. However, the closing attorney represented you as well, so the documents are also your property.

If they ignore the request, you can file a motion with the court to require them to produce the documents. The worst that can happen is that a judge allows them to withhold some material, after making themselves look bad and being thrown off their game in what is supposed to be a simple and pain free process for them.

Once you have the bank's account records to compare with your own, and have reviewed the documents listed above, you should be able to determine whether you have a defense to the foreclosure. If this is the case, I would again urge you to use the time to find legal counsel. These waters are too deep in the litigation pool for most people, however smart, to navigate without experience. I cannot in this book guide you as to how to defend a foreclosure case in court.

Even if there is no obvious defense to the foreclosure action, you should still file responsive pleadings. Simply contesting the case might extend you time in possession of the property by months or years. There is nothing unethical or inappropriate about requiring the bank to produce the original documents that give them the right to take possession, and to document your payment history. The fact that this process takes time is to your advantage.

It is also important to keep careful watch over the litigation process as long as the case is pending. Whether the matter is an eviction or a foreclosure, you do not want to find out that an order is issued by having law enforcement show up at your door, order in hand, to remove you.

If you are fairly certain that you will be remove from the property in the near future, plan ahead. Start moving, taking your most valuable and precious possessions out of the home so that they cannot be seized and sold by the bank, finance company or landlord. This can be done easily before the order is issued, but is almost impossible afterwards.

CHAPTER FOUR: MEDICAL EXPENSES

As everyone knows, we are in a state of extreme uncertainty as to what our health care system will look like in a few years. However, for the time being, we are still dealing with a hybrid of private and government medical entities that works well in many cases, but has some strange characteristics.

These would include the following facts:

1. It is far more expensive to buy your prescriptions or health care services without government benefits, in fact, prohibitively so.
2. It is almost unheard of to inquire about the price of health care services before the services are rendered (unlike any other industry I am aware of.)
3. Doctors are actively lobbied to prescribe certain medications in ways that might strike many of us as inappropriate, when the newer drugs are generally far more expensive than older alternatives which are often safer and more thoroughly evaluated.

4. This places doctors in a position of needing to consider the financial means of the patient when prescribing medications, something they are not trained for and often do not wish to do.

From this, we can draw a few simple conclusions. If you are not comparison shopping, you must start. There is nothing to prevent a consumer from calling up the financial department of a hospital or health services provider and asking what the standard charges would be for certain services. The differences can be dramatic.

Secondly, when the doctor prescribes medication ask questions about costs, especially if you are uninsured. Often, there is a generic alternative, or an older drug that can serve the same purpose at less cost that the newer one that is being aggressively marketed. Don't fool yourself. Doctors are as subject to being manipulated by marketing and salespeople as anyone else. When asked, many will helpfully provide free samples which can save you money.

Take the time to search for coupons, rebates and discounts on the internet for your prescriptions. These can save you hundreds to thousands of dollars. In fact, many offer the opportunity to apply for a hardship petition and be provided the drugs for free. However, keep in mind that this usually involves the cooperation of the treating physician and production of medical records.

If at all possible, avoid the use of internet pharmacies, especially those offering too good to be true discounts. Many of these will offer what is purported to be an on line consultation with a doctor, who is immediately available and ready with prescription pad.

The problem here is that most of the sites are based overseas, unregulated, and have highly questionable quality control standards. You may receive drugs that are past their expiration date, placebos, or even the wrong prescription. While your pharmacist is not infallible, he or she is at least resident in the community, accountable, and concerned about maintaining his or her reputation. That counts for a lot.

Also, if you have Medicare or Medicaid coverage, be aware that there are restrictions as to when and to what extent you can be billed in excess of what the agency pays. The general rule is that if you are a qualified Medicare Beneficiary (QMB), you cannot be billed for services covered under Medicare, even if Medicare refuses to pay for the services. A Qualified Medicare Beneficiary is a person who has an income of less than one hundred percent of the Federal Poverty limit, who is eligible for Medicaid, and pays Medicare premiums, deductibles, and coinsurance for both Part A and Part B.

This is true even if the patient has signed a document agreeing to be liable for the services. Health care providers who violate this provision of the law are subject to sanctions and fines.

Lastly, understand that contrary to what you will be told, everything is negotiable. If you are uninsured or self-insured, you have already been given the short end of the stick. Because of your status, the cost of everything from prescriptions to operating room use to Kleenex has been artificially inflated. Your bill has been padded to levels that no private insurance company, and certainly not any federal agency, would ever agree to pay.

The health care provider is well aware of this. Likewise, it is aware of the probability that you as an uninsured individual cannot afford the unrealistically padded bill, and might default outright on the debt. As such, they are likely to be receptive to an attempt to negotiate a drastic reduction in the amount owed, a minimal monthly payment, or both.

If the idea of attempting to negotiate makes you uncomfortable, find someone to do it for you. While it is not done frequently, it is possible to hire an attorney for this purpose. Alternately, ask a trusted friend or family member with a good understanding of finances to do the dirty work, but understand that you might have to provide documents to the healthcare provider authorizing this person to act on your behalf.

As always, there are essential rules to this process. Insist that any agreement is reduced in writing, and executed by an individual with authority to negotiate, before sending any money. Also, remember that your conversations will be recorded. Any statement you make that admits that you owe the debt can be held against you in a court of law.

CHAPTER FIVE: VEHICLE REPOSSESSIONS

The good news is that, unlike your house, the bank does not want your car. The bad news is that, also unlike your house, your car is mobile. This means that however reluctant the bank might be to take possession, the process is a lot easier.

Almost from the beginning, the law has permitted a creditor to repossess an automobile without a court order provided this was done peacefully. However, through the years, auto repossessions involving street fights, weapons and running people over have been characterized as "peaceful."

The plot of the classic film "Sunset Boulevard" revolves around an automobile repossession. The main character, a down on his luck screen writer, is involved in a high speed chase, fleeing from two men hired to repossess his car and break his legs. To evade them, he turns into the open garage of an old Hollywood mansion and finds a far worse fate.

I highly recommend the movie, but my point is this. Attempting to conceal a vehicle from a credit agency or a repo company is a dangerous game. Innocent people can be seriously hurt, personal property destroyed, and other bad things can happen.

Instead, explore other options. If there is a legal defense which may entitle you to continued possession of the vehicle, use it. Hire an attorney, request the assistance of a neighborhood legal assistance program, or go to the appropriate court yourself. File for an injunction to prevent repossession of the vehicle until your defenses can be heard.

Of course, this is assuming that you want or need to keep the vehicle. If you have little or no equity in your car, and no real chance of being able to make the payments in future, you might be as well off to simply let it go. This is especially true if you have another reliable car, or live in an area with a good public transit system.

The late payments will have already affected your credit rating. Chances are that by the time the situation has become this serious, the damage has already been done. Repairing your credit will be of long term importance, but short term survival is the issue of the moment.

If you are unsure as to whether you have equity in the car, this can be quickly determined. First of all, you will need to find the payoff amount of the loan. The documentation sent to you by the bank or finance company should provide this figure.

If not, contact the creditor and request that you be provided the payoff amount. While you are at it, request a payment history, which you should immediately compare with your own payment book, computer records, or cancelled checks to confirm that you have been properly credited with all payments.

Secondly, you will need to know the value of the car. There are several sites on the web which will provide a relatively accurate estimate. One of the oldest and best is Kelly's Blue Book, which is a principle source for dealers and long predates the internet era.

There are several factors which effect value, so you will need to input some data. The calculations will require the mileage of the vehicle, a fair assessment of condition, and a detailed listing of the optional equipment on the car.

You will then be given the option of calculating the Retail value, Wholesale value, or trade in value. Since you are trying to make an objective decision as to whether to attempt to keep the vehicle, you will want a conservative valuation. Look at the "trade in" value, which is the figure you would get trading the car in at a dealership.

After you have the two figures, simply subtract the payoff amount of the loan from the value of the car. Unfortunately, most loans are structured so that the first several years of payments are applied heavily toward interest. For this reason, there is a good chance that you will have no equity in your car.

Also, keep in mind that as the vehicle ages, adding mileage, wear, and tear, your equity in the vehicle will slowly disappear. This calculation should allow you to determine whether your automobile has any value as an asset, as opposed to simply the pleasure and convenience of driving it. The result might motivate you to raise the necessary cash, or alternately, at least provide some comfort if this is not possible.

It is also worth noting that it is possible to sue a bank, finance company, or repo company for wrongful repossession of a vehicle. There are various theories by which this can be done, including but not limited to fraud, negligence in accounting, violation of federal or state credit laws, or illegal conduct and practices during the act of repossession.

Likewise, any unlawful and injurious acts which occur during and in consequence of the repossession can also provide the basis for a lawsuit. For example, if a person attempts to prevent a stranger who does not identify him or herself from driving off in his car, and is injured, this might result in a civil lawsuit and possibly criminal prosecution.

However to repeat, it is important to understand that the bank does not want your car. A repossessed car is inevitably sold at auction for pennies on the dollar, with the proceeds applied toward the unpaid balance on the loan. From there, the bank is left to attempt to collect the balance from an angry and disgruntled customer who probably lost his job about the same time as he lost his wheels. The result is no better for the creditor than the debtor.

There is a real possibility of working things out with the bank or finance company. For advice as to how to proceed, review the discussion in Chapter Three regarding foreclosure. Keep in mind that any agreement to reduce or modify a payment schedule should be in writing, signed by an employee of the creditor with authority to enter into the agreement. No payment should be made until the agreement has been reduced into writing.

CHAPTER SIX: TAX TIPS.

The Internal Revenue Service, and its state and local equivalents, are unique among the entities discussed in this book. The Banks, Finance Companies, and other creditors have considerable resources which can be used to great advantage against members of the general public, but are often limited in what they can do by local, state, or federal law.

The various tax agencies, on the other hand, have virtually *unlimited* resources, and virtually *zero* accountability. The quality and competence of particular agency employees might vary dramatically, but this hardly matters. Your opponent is able to rewrite the rules as the game goes along. It cannot be outsmarted, or outlasted.

So what can be done? There is a booming industry which exists for the purpose of answering just this question. Long careers have been spent interpreting the tax code which are is constantly being rewritten by anonymous bureaucrats with little or no supervision. It sometimes seems that every other ad on radio or television is hawking the services of a tax attorney or tax defense business.

One thing is certain. The testimonials which claim that these businesses can magically solve a serious tax problem with a few phone calls are nonsense. So are the accounts of a "taxpayer amnesty" of some sort during which the Internal Revenue Services is writing off penalties and interest on unpaid taxes like so many drunken sailors.

Does this mean you should go this alone? No. There is a serious risk of making the situation worse, just by picking up the phone and making a call. As mentioned earlier, statements made to a finance company, credit bureau, or collection agency can dramatically affect your rights in court.

In the case of a tax issue, there is a far worse possibility. Your attempt to settle an issue regarding a minor tax penalty, for example, might trigger a full audit of your tax return. This might occur not only because of what you say, but is equally likely to occur simply because the agent you spoke with thought you were rude or disrespectful.

If the amount of the fine or penalty is relatively small, simply pay it and live to fight another day. If this is not possible, consider writing the tax agency in question and requesting a payment schedule to resolve the issue. In many cases, this ends with a better result than would occur from a prolonged fight.

Should the situation go beyond this, hire the best legal counsel you can afford. Ideally, this would be an attorney certified as a tax specialist. There are stringent requirements for an attorney to be allowed to characterize him or herself as a specialist, and to maintain that distinction.

Of course, such help does not come cheap. If this is impossible for you, consider contacting your local elected officials, who often have staff members able to assist constituents with these problems.

Alternately, if you engaged the services of a tax preparation firm, you might be entitled to assistance should issues arise related to the return. If you choose to seek assistance from this source, be aware that there is a conflict of interest. The agency that prepared the return does not want to be liable to you for negligent preparation of the return, or criminally liable to the government for abetting your tax fraud. Those concerns will be primary, and protecting you a distant secondary concern.

Here are a few sound rules to keep in mind when dealing with a tax agency:

1. If at all possible, avoid in person or direct telephone contact with the tax agency. This opens the possibility of a broader fishing expedition, which could be potentially catastrophic. If you are forced to deal with a tax agency under these circumstances, ALWAYS;

    a. Keep your calm and be polite;
    b. Listen to the question you are being asked;
    c. Ask that it be repeated if you do not hear or understand;
    d. Provide short, responsive answers and no information unresponsive to the question.

This does not mean that you have to be cold and personality free. I once had to speak with an IRS agent about a relatively minor tax penalty. There were no skeletons in my closet, but I did not care to spend hours or years of my future time proving this. I was understandably nervous, and it showed.

The question was involved deductions for certain office expenses. I calmly explained the circumstances, explaining how the items were replacements for equipment that had been destroyed in my car during an accident. When I had finished, the agent asked me if I had lost anything else as a result of the incident. Without thinking, I said:

"Well, I'm pretty sure I'll never wear this pair of underwear again."

She laughed, and mentioned that this was the first time she had laughed all day.

2. Consider providing verified testimony as to the issue in question. Despite the resources available to the Internal Revenue Service and to state and local tax agencies, only a small percentage of tax cases are actively investigated. Prepare a sworn affidavit of your testimony with regards to the issue in question. It will in all probability be the only sworn testimony in your file, and consequentially the unopposed findings of fact in your case.

   This advice comes with a word of caution. Understand that whatever information you present to any federal, state, or local tax agency is consider to be presented under oath, and thus, a potential basis for a criminal prosecution.

   Perjury prosecutions are rare, but attorneys representing Barry Bonds and Roger Clements probably considered their clients safe at the time. In other words, do not lie under oath, and shy away from making questionable statements that cannot be corroborated with documents or other evidence already in your possession.

3. Watch for deadlines. It is good practice to read any correspondence from a tax agency at least three times. If there is a deadline to respond, understand that missing it can be fatal to your claim. When you find a deadline, calendar it in your computer, smart phone, or do it the old fashioned way and write it

down in a note pad. Where there is a deadline, plan to complete the required action at least five days before that date. Keep in mind that life happens and gets in the way.

4. The best way to win an argument with a tax agency is with documents. When you received notice of an audit, or a tax penalty you intend to contest, contact your bank, accountant, tax preparer, or anyone else who has possession of your bank statements, checks, receipts, or other records. Go ahead and begin the tedious process of plowing through this material to find what you need, knowing that all the tedium will turn into satisfaction when you find the smoking gun.

5. To be proactive, get in the habit of scanning every receipt, check, photograph, or other document which verifies a deduction on your return, or verifies income. If these documents are attached to the return at the time, and well organized, your work is already done. You might even consider attaching the documents to your return when it is mailed to the agency, thus offering proof before a question is ever raised.

CHAPTER SEVEN: TITHING.

You also have a financial obligation to your faith. This is an issue that many Christians wrestle with in these difficult times. There is ample room to debate just what satisfies the obligation, however, its existence cannot be denied.

Bring the whole into the storehouse that there may be food in my house. Test me in this-says the LORD ALMIGHTY-and see if I **will not throw open the floodgates of heaven and pour out so much blessing that there will not be room enough for it.**

Malachi 3:10

A tithe of everything from the land, whether grain from the soil or fruit from the trees belongs to the LORD, **It is held for the LORD.**

Leviticus 27:30

The bookkeeper in us might first notice the clarity and simplicity of the tax system decried by the Supreme Being. There could be no more stark contrast to the muddled mess imposed on us by secular government. It is simple enough to understand that since most of us no longer till the soil, a monetary contribution is to be expected.

However, the verses do not address one basic question that would have been equally pertinent in Biblical times. A tithe by definition is ten percent of something. However, is this ten percent to be calculated based upon a GROSS or NET calculation of an individual's wealth?

This appears to remain as an issue of conscience, although the phrase "Bring the whole to the storehouse.." seems to imply that the share would be taken off the top. Historically, the Romans were every bit as aggressive in collection taxes as any modern state; and certainly far more brutal in punishing tax cheats. Yet the verse does not imply that the emperor or any secular government would take precedence, nor would any Christian suggest otherwise upon careful thought.

Can the tithe be provided in non-monetary forms? Again, whether good works for the church or other religious organizations could be applied towards the tithe is a matter of opinion. It would seem a reasonable argument that time devoted to God's work might be considered a contribution to tithe. What, when, and to what extent again are matters for debate.

However, it is only appropriate to remind the reader that a primary creditor exists, who has provided all that we have. Each individual must address this issue as a matter of conscience, knowing that his or her choice will be one day subject to review.

Fortunately, tithes are tax deductible. However, in recent years, the Internal Revenue Service has on occasion relied on technicalities in the code to deny the deduction. For example, in Durden vs. Commissioner, TC memo 2012-140 US Tax Court, the Commission denied a large deduction to a tithing couple, despite conceding that the tithes were undisputedly paid to the church.

The commission, and ultimately the court, based its opinion upon a strict adherence to the terms of IRS Code Sections 170 (A) (B) and (C). Those provisions require the recipient church to issue a special receipt which must contain the following information:

1. The amount or value of the donation;
2. A description of anything given in return for the donation;
3. The value of anything given in return for the donation;
4. The receipt must have been issue prior to the time of filing and claim of the deduction.

Sadly, in the Darden case, the original receipt issue by the court did not meet these requirements. After the deduction was denied, the church issued a new receipt intended to satisfy the requirements of the code provision. Because this receipt was not issued prior to the date at which the deduction was claimed, it did not cure the defect.

While the opinion has no language to suggest such, one wonders whether the choices of the Commission in this case are reflective of a change in attitude towards religious organizations in general and Christian groups in particular.

Fortunately, there is constitutional protection for the deductibility of tithes. For the present, be confident that the deduction will remain in place, but anticipate traps for the unwary intended to deprive churchgoers of their rights on technical grounds.

CONCLUSION

Wealth and honor come from you. You are the ruler of all things. In your

hands are strength and power to exalt and give strength to all.

1 Chronicles 29:12

www.ingramcontent.com/pod-product-compliance
Lightning Source LLC
Chambersburg PA
CBHW070721180526
45167CB00004B/1563